Finland's Flags and the National Coat of Arms

National flag

National Coat of Arms

State flag (rectangular)

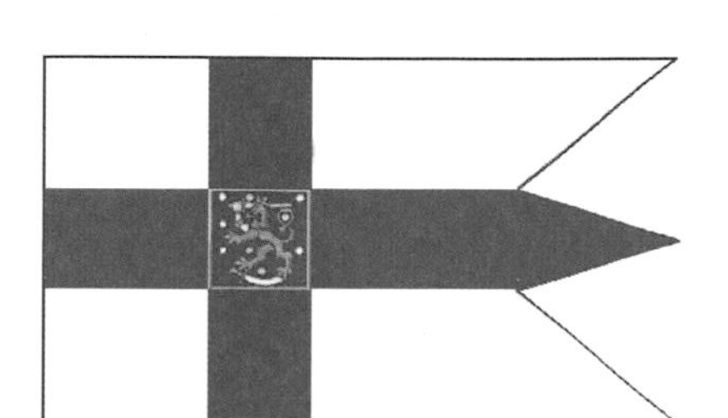

State flag (with edge)

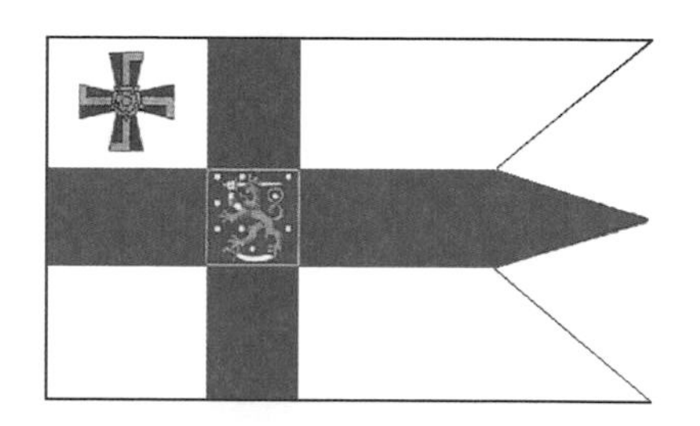

Presidential flag

Flag of Åland

Sami flag

Coats of Arms of the Finnish Counties

Southern Finland

Eastern Finland

Western Finland

Oulu

Lapland

Coats of Arms of Finland's biggest cities

Helsinki

Espoo

Tampere

Vantaa

Turku

English edition

Raimo Suikkari

FINLAND
today

English edition

Raimo Suikkari

Photo sources:
ABB Industry Group: page 10 (centre)
Comma Pictures/Delany Brendany: 9 (top)
Comma Pictures/Tolvanen Lauri: 19
Comma Pictures/Palsila Kari: 48 and 60
Comma Pictures/Kolho Matti: 58 (left)
Comma Pictures/Jormanainen Juha: 80–81
Comma Pictures/Palsila Kari: 59 (centre)
Comma Pictures/Edvardsson Tom: 51 (centre, left)
Fregatti Oy: 61
Honkamajat Finland Oy Ltd: 13 (centre)
Ii-circuit Oy: 11 (top)
Indav Ltd: 29 (bottom)
Innopoli: 15 (bottom)
Ingervo Eeva and Pertti: 20 (bottom)
Kalevala Koru Oy: 62 (top)
Kangas Pentti-Oskari: 40
Karjanoja Matti: 24
Klemelä Leena: 38
Kone Oy: 2 (bottom)
Konsertti- ja kongressitalo Mikaeli: 57 (top)
Koski Kari: 85 (bottom)
Kuvasuomi Ky/Matti Kolho: 36 (top)
Kuvataiteen keskusarkisto: 29 (top 30–31)
Kylpylä Kivitippu: 57 (centre and bottom)
Kärki Liisa, Oulu University: 11 (centre)
Lahden kaupungin matkailutoimisto: 46 (bottom)
Laine Risto: 11 (bottom)
Lehtikuva Oy: 41
Lehtikuva Oy/Kenneth Johansson: 43
Lehtikuva Oy/Erkki Laitila: 42
Lehtikuva Oy/AP Photo/Michel Éuler 43
Lehtikuva Oy/Jussi Nukari: 44
Lehtikuva Oy/Pekka Sakki: 34
Lehtikuva Oy/Heikki Saukonmaa: 47 (centre)
Lehtikuva Oy/Markku Ulander: 14
Lehtikuva Oy/ Tor Wennström: 52 and 59
Lentokuva Vallas Oy: 52 (bottom) and 58 (bottom) (LKA)
Lomaliitto ry: page 53 (bottom)
Martikkala Timo/LKA: page 88
Mylius Gero/Indav Ltd: page 10
Nokia: cover page (bottom) 12 (top) and 26
Rista Simo: 21
SA-kuva: 19 (centre)
Salminen Reijo/LKA: 72
Scandic Hotel Kajaani: 53 (top)
Seinäjoki polytechnic: 9 (bottom)
Sibelius Museum: 35 (right)
Sirén Gallen-Kallela Aivi: 28, 32–33
Suikkari, Helena: 96
Studio Juha Sarkkinen: 11 (centre and bottom)
Suikkari Jouko: 59 (top), 66 (bottom) 82 (bottom) and 83
SRM: 22
Tampereen kylpylä: 54
Taskinen Juha/LKA: 75 (top)
Träskelin Rauno/SRM: 22 and 23
Tulokas Merja: 12 (bottom)
Turku University: 8
Valmet: 13 (top)
Venhola Eero: 21 (bottom)

Data sources:
Matti Kohva (EU-info)
Statistics Finland
Sonera, telecommunication statistics

Original text, photographs and implementation: Raimo Suikkari
Other photographs: see photo sources

Layout: Maria Wallin
English text: Marianne Lindahl
Publisher: RKS Tietopalvelu Oy
Printed by Karisto Oy, Hämeenlinna, 2002
4th edition
Hardbound ISBN 951-97775-6-3
Paperback ISBN 952-5308-00-6

This book has been published without outside financial support or grants.

Introduction

International comparisons show that Finland ranks among the leading countries in the world as far as scientific and economic competitiveness are concerned. This achievement is the result of hard and persistent work of many generations. Finland's outstanding know-how and advanced technology is recognized all over the world. The spectacular seasonal changes in the unspoiled Finnish landscape is an important source of inspiration for the creative and dynamic Finnish people.

In different areas of culture, a new generation of artists, musicians and writers continue in the footsteps of world celebrities such as composer Jean Sibelius and painter Akseli Gallen-Kallela. Today's young Finnish athletes follow the example of legendary long distance runner Paavo Nurmi.

Finland is an active member of the European Union, and the country's work for peace is widely recognized. I hope that this book will give its readers a vision of Finland as a dynamic, modern country, confidently facing the challenges of a new millennium.

Raimo Suikkari

KIASMA
Aavan
tällä
KIASMA
live

Kiasma, the Museum of Contemporary Art, was completed in 1998. This modern building is a combined living room, cultural centre and museum, incorporating contemporary art, multimedia and the Kiasma-theatre. The building was designed by the American architect Steven Holl.

Pageant of honorary and graduated doctors of the Turku University approaching the Turku cathedral.

Education – a Number One Priority

Education has a high priority in Finland. Already at comprehensive schools, Finnish children study two foreign languages besides their mother tongue. The possibilities for postgradual studies are excellent, and far-sighted enterprises sponsor the education of young, promising students. Every year, an impressive number of Finns pass the immatriculation exam.

There are universities in all major Finnish cities, the northernmost being situated in Rovaniemi in Lapland.

A multitude of different adult eduction programmes create vast opportunities for lifelong learning and complementary studies.

Thanks to Finland's high educational level and advanced technology, the employment situation in the country has improved considerably over the past years.

Students at Seinäjoki Polytechnic are trained for demanding positions in the fields of technology, trade, the health and social sectors, natural resources, culture and catering. This building incorporates the school's economics and business department.

The world's biggest aluminium catamaran "Stena Explorer" and its two sister vessels have been built at the Aker Finnyards shipyard in Rauma. This passenger and car ferry, able to carry 1 500 persons and 375 cars, has been called "a high-rise block of flats advancing at 40 knots".

AZIPOD is a new propeller system developed in Finland. In this system, an electric motor is placed in a rotating propeller unit. No rudder is needed, and the fuel consumption is low.

The international energy and chemicals company Fortum Oyj is known for its pro-environment product strategy. It was the first company in Europe to start production of cleaner fuels for traffic and industry. Fortum has operations in more than 30 countries. Over 90% of the company's production is certified according to environmental standards. The picture shows Fortum's head office building at Keilaniemi in Espoo.

Finnish Specialists Create Top Technology

Finnish technology and technical know-how has made outstanding international achievements in many fields. Finnish space technology innovations are used in several international projects.

Finnish companies and research institutes participate in the development and manufacture of equipment for twelve satellites, the NASA space shuttle and an international space station. The fields of ozone layer research and space sector industry are constantly developing.

Finnish achievements in the fields of data processing, solar energy, ultralow temperature physics, electronics, wood processing and paper industry as well as shuipbuilding are recognized all over the world. Thanks to a flexible and efficient research cooperation between the industry and the universitites, Finland has become one of the world leaders in technology development and applications. The digital revolution is likely to lead to a considerable breakthrough in Finland, economically as well as socially. Finland is a modern, dynamic information society, and it is constantly developing its advanced technology.

The scope of this book only allows a presentation of a few of the numerous examples of Finnish dynamism, entrepreneurship and creativity:

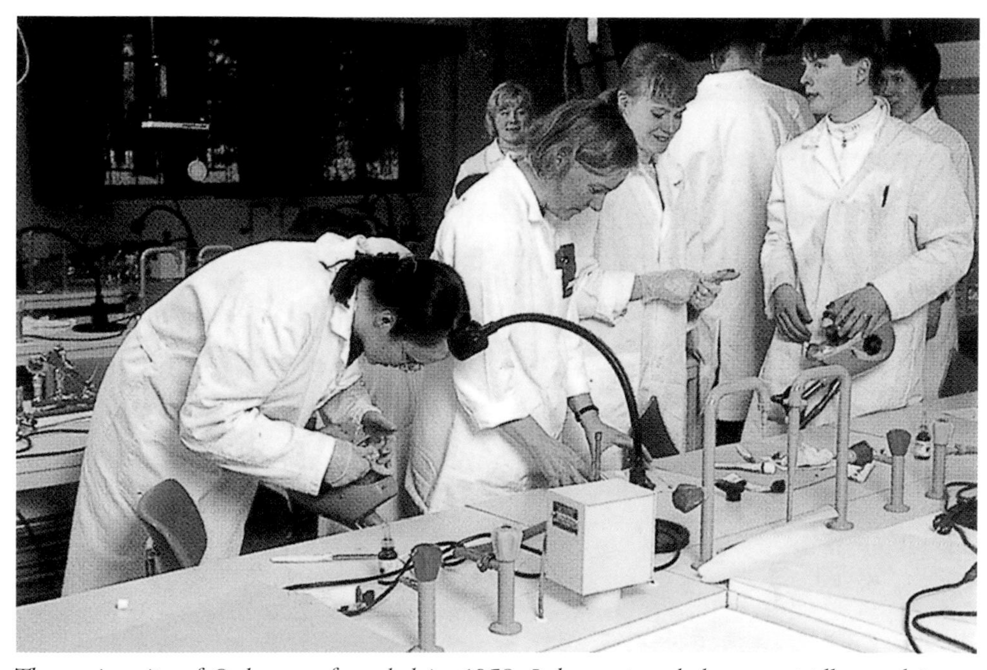

The university of Oulu was founded in 1958. It has expanded very rapidly, and is now one of the leading universities in Finland. The university operates in eight major fields; humanities, education, economics, natural sciences, technology (including architecture), medicine, dentistry (see photo) and health care, distributed on five faculties.

Oy Sisu Auto Ab is a company manufacturing heavy trucks for demanding customer groups requiring special product characteristics. The company is known for its customer orientated, efficient and flexible way of operating. Sisu Auto is the only European manufacturer using engines and transmissions from different suppliers in its product range. Each truck is made by selecting the best possible components, taking into account that in modern trucks the most important properties are efficiency, economy and payload.

Nokia is a broad-scope communications company offering high technology with a human touch. The company is a world leader in wireless data infrastructure solutions. A pioneer in mobile telephony, Nokia is a leading global company focussed on the key growth areas of wireline and wireless telecommunications. Nokia's goal is to simplify the technology, yet still offer feature-rich products to anticipate future needs. The company strives for continued leadership in the fastest growing telecommunications segments, through speed in anticipating and fulfilling customer and consumer needs, quality in products and processes, as well as openness with people and their new ideas.

Rotating Actuator for Cassini Plasma Spectrometer CAPS

The Cassini spacecraft on its way to Saturn will study the planet, its rings and moons and its magnetosphere. VTT Automation provided two Rotating Actuators for the Cassini Mission launched in 1997. CAPS is one of the instruments on board Cassini. The instrument will begin operation in the year 2004, when the spacecraft goes into orbit around Saturn, and it will work until 2008. The rotating mechanism is built to survive the spacecraft launch vibration, and to operate in the space environment for 11 years with minimal resources and no maintenance.

Metso Oyj is the world leading manufacturer of paper and paperboard machines. Metso's product range also comprises automation technology, air and heat management during the papermaking process and mechanical drive components, among other products. The operations of the Metso group are based on a worldwide production network and flexible and efficient team work. Metso gives high priority to its environmental responsibility in its own production as well as in the processes offered to the customers.

About 70 % of Finland's land area is virgin forest. The Metla Forest Research Institute owns about 148 000 hectares of forests, of which 68 000 hectares is under protection. Metla provides scientific information regarding the forest environment, different forms of forest use as well as forestry economy.

In Finland, the monitoring of woodworking machinery systems is integrated into the international AMAP-programme and the TIMES-database.

The aim of the close follow-up of the forest eco-systems is to produce detailed information about the relation between forest health, air pollution and other stress factors.

This house representing the product range of Oy Honkamajat Finland Ltd is an excellent example of Finnish timber construction know-how.

KÄMP

Adjacent to Kämp Hotel there is a modern shopping centre, the Kämp Gallery, with stylish cafés and leading fashion and desing shops under a beautiful glass cupola.

Finland has many historically and architecturally valuable sights. The neorenaissance building incorporation Kämp Hotel in Pohjoisesplanadi streeet was desingned by Karl Theodor Höijer, and completed in 1887. It has recently been restored to its original appearance. Kämp Hotel is a first class luxyry hotel, favoured by foreign businessmen and celebrities.

Outlines of Finland's History – From the Ice Age to Present Times

Finland was probably inhabited already before the Ice Age, and reinhabited shortly after the glaciers had retreated and the land risen above the see. In those days, people depended on hunting and fishing. The Iron Age (500 BC –1200 AC) saw the spread and development of agriculture.

Christianity reached Finland in the 13th century. The city of Turku became the country's episcopal and administrative centre.

In the 1520s, the Reformation set in motion a great rise in Finnish-language culture. The Bishop of Turku, Mikael Agricola, translated the New Testament into Finnish and created written Finnish. In the 17th century, while still being a part of the Swedish kingdom, Finland was involved in many wars. In 1721, Russia conquered vast areas of southeastern Finland, and after the war of 1808–1809, occupied the whole country. Finland now became an autonomous Grand Duchy of Russia. However, the laws and administration established under the Swedish rule remained in force.

In the 19th century, the Finnish national movement gained momentum. The national epic, Kalevala, compiled by Elias Lönnrot, was published in 1835, and the patriotic poetry of J.L. Runeberg was hailed with enthusiasm. The end of the19th century saw the beginning of industrialisation, economic upswing and population growth.

In 1917, the October revolution broke out in Russia, and Finland declared its independence on 6 December 1917. The political unrest in the country led to a civil war between the "Reds" representing the radical wing of the social democratic party and the "Whites" supporting the government and the conservatives. The civil war ended in May 1918 with the victory of the government troops.

When Finland refused to allow the Soviet Union to build military bases on its territory, the Soviet Union attacked Finland in November 1939. This so called "Winter War" ended in March 1940. The war continued from 1941 to 1944, and Finland had to yield vast territories to the Soviet Union, and pay heavy war reparations until 1952.

During the presidency of J.K. Paasikivi, a Treaty of Friendship, Cooperation and Mutual Assistance was signed with the Soviet Union in 1947. However, Finland continued its policy of active neutrality. In 1955, Finland became a member of the United Nations.

In 1956, Urho Kekkonen was elected president. He was the driving force behind the Conference on Security and Cooperation in Europe, held in Helsinki in summer 1975. During his time in office, which comprised a quarter of a century, Finland developed into an urban, industrialised and service-centered nation. A free-trade agreement with the EEC was signed in 1973.

In 1981, Mauno Koivisto succeeded Urho Kekkonen as president. During his presidency Finland became a full member of EFTA, and started negotiations about membership in the European Union. In 1994, Martti Ahtisaari was elected the 10th president of the Republic of Finland. In the year 2000 he was succeeded by Tarja Halonen, the first woman in Finland's history to occupy this office. In 1995, following a referendum, Finland became a member of EU.

The foundation-stones of the Turku castle originate from the 13th century. As a historical museum, the castle is a popular tourist attraction (right).

The church of the Suomenlinna fortress islands off the coast of Helsinki was built in the 1860s. Originally, it was an Orthodox temple called the Alexander Nevski church. Today it is a Lutheran church.

Defense and Peacekeeping

Finland has compulsory military service. The basic elements of Finnish security policy are an independent and trustworthy defence force and membership in the European Union.

Membership of thc European Union has added clarity and strength to Finland's international position as a part of a community of democratic states. A central goal for Finland is to expand this cooperation, and to contribute towards consolidating security in Northern Europe and the Baltic Sea region.

Participation in UN peacekeeping operations is the most prominent element of Finland's international military cooperation. During the past forty years, Finland has sent 35 000 participants to peacekeeping missions in different parts of the world. Several Finnish officers occupy high international management positions.

The President of the Republic is the Commander-in-Chief of the Finnish defense forces. The leader of the defense forces is the Chief of Defense, reporting directly to the president.

In peacetime, the Air Force is responsible for the continuous monitoring of the air space. The picture shows one of the recently acquired Hornet fighters.

Finnish soldiers marching in Helsinki.

"Oulu" the missile-carrying vessel of the Marine Force patroling the coastline of Turku. The ship's radars cover the whole area of the Gulf of Finland.

Finnish Architecture and Alvar Aalto

In the olden days, Finns used wood as building material for their houses, mainly logs from pine wood. Self-learned folk masters built wooden churches, the Petäjävesi church being one of the most famous houses of worship from this time. In the Middle Age, greystone was a popular construction material for churches and castles, such as the Olavinlinna fortress and the castles of Turku and Wyborg.

Carl Ludwig Engel was one of the most famous representatives of 19th century neoclassical style architecture. He planned the Lutheran Cathedral and other imposing buildings around the Senate House Square in Helsinki, a rare example of stylistic continuity.

During the second half of the 19th century, functions, technology and styles diversified. The neo-gothic style gained its greatest popularity in ecclesiastical architecture. The red-brick architecture of the riverside buildings of the industrial city of Tampere reflects the intensity of industrialisation. Among the most famous examples of 20th century National-Romantic style is Hvitträsk, at Kirkkonummi, close to Helsinki, a shared living and studio space built in 1903 by architects Eliel Saarinen, Herman Gesellius and Armas Lindgren.

During the period that followed Finland's independence, a new classicism became the dominant style in architecture. The House of Parliament in Helsinki designed by J.S. Sirén, and completed in the 1930s is a typical example of this style.

Alvar Aalto is undoubtedly the most celebrated among Finnish architects. He can be described as one of our century´s landmarks in architecture. One of his first masterpieces of functionalism is the Paimio Tuberculosis Sanatorium. The best known among his later works are the Finlandia Hall in Helsinki and the Opera House in Essen, Germany. In his works, Alvar Aalto always aimed at a holistic conception of space.

Other famous post-war Finnish architects are Raili and Reima Pietilä, creators of the City Library in Tampere, among other buildings.

The facade material of the Finlandia Hall, designed by Alvar Aalto, is marble. The building, completed in 1971, is one of his latest creations.

Alvar and Elissa Aalto

Finlandia Hall interior details. The freely designed ceiling and walls form an independent sculptural masterpiece, and yet they are an essential part of the architecture. The spacious entrance hall – piazzo – was also designed by Alvar Aalto.

Alvar Aalto has also become famous as a furniture designer. He developed wooden furniture with laminated and moulded birchwood structures and curved plywood seats, the curves of which resembled the lines of his famous glass vase, designed in 1937.

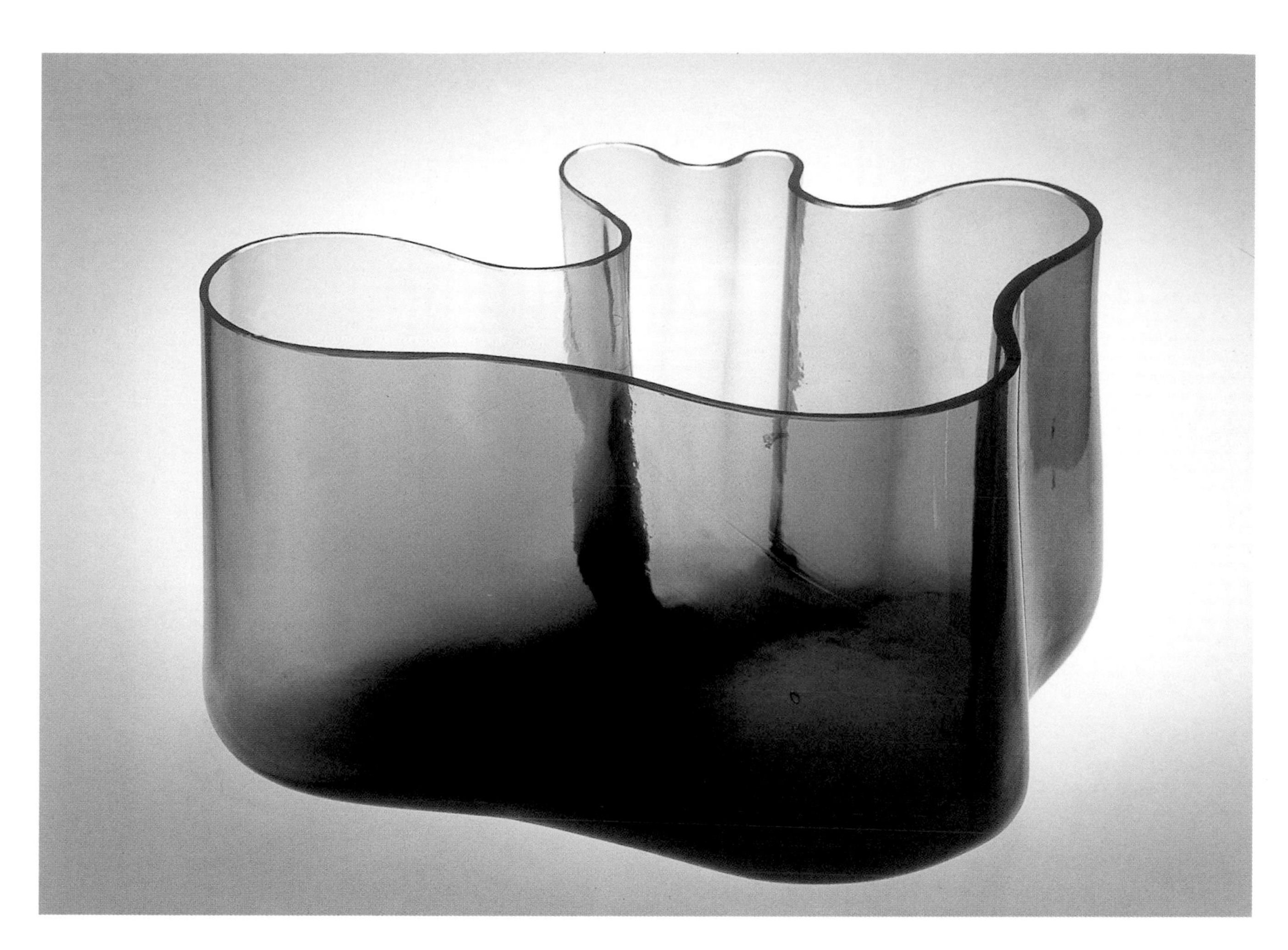

Wooden houses have experienced a come-back. The heritage of Alvar Aalto is continued by innovative architects like Mikko Kaira, who has designed the "Misteli" day care centre in Vantaa near Helsinki. When the sun is shining, the shades of the grating create their own playful pattern in the spacious playground in the main hall.

The Kerimäki church in South Savo was built in 1847. It is the biggest wooden church in Finland. It was planned by E.B. Lohrman and A.E. Granstedt.

The Tampere city library, designed by Raili and Reima Pietilä, was completed in 1986. Seen from above, the building looks like a bird, but the basic structural idea is that of a shell. The interior colours are inspired by the Finnish landscape.

The Nokia-house at Keilalahti in Espoo, completed in 1997, is designed by Pekka Helin. The interior design is by Iiris Ulin. The transparent building is covered with an energy saving glass facade. Whenever possible, natural materials have been used in the furnishings. The double facade won a facade prize in 1997. This building is the work place for over one thousand Nokia-employees, and a central meeting place for Nokia's clients from all over the world.

The Paimio hospital designed by Alvar Aalto was completed in 1933. (right).

The national-romantic Kalevala paintings and graphics have placed Akseli Gallen-Kallela (1865–1931) in a unique position in the history of Finnish art. This painting, "The Woodpecker", is from 1893.

Finnish Art in a Nutshell

The most ancient examples of Finnish painting are many thousand years old. Evidence of this can still be seen for example in rock paintings depicting elk heads. The oldest mural paintings in stone churches are from the 15th century. Secular paintings such as portraits appeared alongside church paintings around the 17th century.

Among the most distuinguished 18th century painters were the rococo-inspired portraitist Isac Wacklin and Nils Schillmark, who specialized in exquisite Gustavian still-life paintings. Leading 19th century artists were the von Wright brothers, masters of romantic landscapes and naturalistic bird paintings, and the realist landscape painter Werner Holmberg.

In the late 19th and early 20th century, the landscape painter and bold colourist Fanny Churberg paved the way for her illustrious "sisters", such as Maria Wiik and Helene Schjerfbeck, who was to become one of the world's most appreciated female painters. Albert Edelfelt, a favourite of the Paris Salons, brough impressionism and outdoor-painting to Finland. Victor Westerholm was another famous outdoor painter of this period. The master of Kalevala-motifs, Akseli Gallen-Kallela, created Finland's most remarkable national pictorial work. Another representative of this period in Finnish art called the "Golden Age" was the individual symbolist painter Hugo Simberg, who cultivated a naïvist style and themes from folk-tales. The predominant realists of this period were Juho Rissanen, a master in depicting ordinary people, and Pekka Halonen, a skilled and fluid winter landscape specialist. Famous colourists representing symbolism were Ellen Thesleff and Magnus Enckell.

One of the earliest 20th century surrealists was Otto Mäkilä, who was later followed by the bold modernist Sam Vanni. The neo-realistic school of the 1970s is represented by Veikko Vionoja.

Besides Alvar Aalto, the best known names in Finnish industrial art are Timo Sarpaneva and Kaj Franck.

Ellen Thesleff emphasized lyricism and drama in her paintings. Her dream-like portraits and landscapes represent a symbolistic and unique colour fantasy. Ellen Thesleff (1869–1954) Self Portrait: 1916, The Finnish National Gallery, Helsinki.

Designer Kaj Franck (1911–1989) has become famous as an innovator of household ware design. He was a precursor for coming designer generations. According to his philisophy, designer articles have to be so practical and easy to use that nobody pays any special attention to them. This idea is demonstrated in his Teema and Kartio series designed for Arabia and Iittala.

Ernst Mether-Borgström was one of the pioneers of Finnish constructivism. His abstract paintings are based on intuition, and emphasize values of colour and form. Ernst Mether-Borgström (1917 –1996) October IV/ 1981, Kiasma, the Museum of Contemporary Art.

Akseli Gallen-Kallela's tempera painting "Kullervo's Departure for War" 1901. The Finnish National Gallery.

Finnish soprano singer Karita Mattila has sung on almost all the worlds operatic stages.

Finland – the Land of Music

Music has long traditions in Finland. About thousand years ago, ancient Kalevala-songs were sung by rune-singers.

The best known Finnish composer, both nationally and internationally is Jean Sibelius (1865–1957). His extensive production includes seven symphonies, numerous symphonic poems, a violin concerto and several orchestral suites. Jean Sibelius is one of the world's most celebrated 20th century symphonic composers.

During the past two decades, Finnish opera has gained international recognition. Aulis Sallinen, Joonas Kokkonen, Einojuhani Rautavaara and Erik Bergman are the most prominent among Finnish opera composers. International stars among Finnish opera singers are Karita Mattila, Soile Isokoski, Monica Groop, Jorma Hynninen and Matti Salminen. Violinist Pekka Kuusisto represents the younger generation of famous Finnish musicians. The genius of conductors like Esa-Pekka Salonen, Okko Kamu, Leif Segerstam, Jorma Panula and Paavo Berglund is recognized all over the world. Internationally renowned Finnish pianists are Ralph Gothoni and Olli Mustonen.

The Savonlinna Opera Festival, arranged in July every year, is an extremely popular event. The vast stone courtyard of the Olavinlinna fortress forms an exotic framework for the opera performances.

The National Opera moved to a modern and purposeful opera house in 1993, and this has further increased the passion for opera that is typical for the Finnish audience.

An extensive network of music schools teach music to as many as 50.000 children. In summer, numerous music festivals attract international visitors every year.

Ainola, the home of Jean and Aino Sibelius in Järvenpää, is now a popular museum. Here Sibelius composed most of his works.

The Sibelius-monument in Helsinki, sculpted by Professor Eila Hiltunen in 1967, is one of Helsinki's most popular tourist attractions.

Jean Sibelius (1865–1957) is one of the most celebrated composers in Finland and in the entire world.

The massive Olavinlinna fortress provides an imposing framework for the annual Opera Festival event.

A scene from the ballet "Giselle" at the National Opera (right). Choregraphy by Sylvie Guillem (according to Coralli, Perrot, Petipa).

Theatre – a Popular Entertainment

The role of the theatre is to offer the audience exciting and aestetic experiences, and make them forget the routines of everyday life. This is a task that the Finnish theatre has been fulfilling to perfection since 1872, the year of the foundation of the Finnish Theatre, which later became the Finnish National Theatre. Finland has nearly 50 theatres fairly evenly distributed in the biggest cities and towns. New generations of actors, directors, dramatists, technical directors and dancers are trained at the Theatre Academy, which was founded in 1943, and gained university status in 1979. Actors are also trained at the drama department of the University of Tampere.

International plays soon found their way to the Finnish theatres, and many Finnish plays have gained popularity abroad. Besides the major theatres, there are many small establishments specializing in intimate and experimental drama.

The multitude of amateur and summer stages show that the Finns really appreciate their theatres.

Among the most famous modern theatre directors are Jouko Turkka, Mikko Majanlahti, Ralf Långbacka and Kalle Holmberg.

The Finnish National Theatre, near the Helsinki Railway Station, was designed by architect Onni Tarjanne, and completed in 1902.

The play "Niskavuoren Heta" by Hella Wuolijoki is as popular today as it was in the 1930s. It is one of the permanent features of the repertoire at the Finnish National Theatre. Here we see Katariina Kaitue in the leading role (left).

A Review of Finnish Literature

The oldest Finnish literature was Finnish-language folk poetry which was preserved in oral tradition. These poems by rune-singers were later compiled by Elias Lönnrot (during 1835–49) into the Finnish national epic "Kalevala".

The first book printed in Finland is the "Missale Aboense" the latin language missal used by the Diocese of Turku. The first books in the Finnish language were published by the Bishop of Turku, Mikael Agricola, about 1540.

Johan Ludwig Runeberg wrote the heroic romances "Tales of Ensign Stål" in 1848–1860. Zacharias Topelius produced a great deal of children's stories and children's plays that has become popular in many parts of the world. The most prominent Finnish writer in the latter half of the 19th century was Aleksis Kivi, the pioneer of Finnish-language novel and drama. His most famous novel is "Seven Brothers", published in 1870. Realism and naturalism, typical for the 1880s is represented by playwright Minna Canth and novelist Juhani Aho. In the 1890s, Eino Leino created his legendary reputation as an idealistic and sensuous poet. The leading 20th century prosaist was Frans-Emil Sillanpää who became the only Finnish writer, to date, to be awarded the Nobel Prize for Literature (1939).

In the 1940's, Mika Waltari wrote his famous novel "The Egyptian" which was to become his international breakthrough. It has been translated into several languages.

In 1954, Väinö Linna published "The Unknown Soldier", the most famous book ever written about our wars. The novel was later made into a monumental film by actor/director Edvin Laine. Linna's famous novel trilogy "Here Beneath the North Star" was published in 1959–1962.

Among the most illustious contemporary writers are Paavo Haavikko, Veijo Meri, Arto Paasilinna, Bo Karpelan, Eeva Kilpi, Tove Jansson and Risto Ahti. Writers reflect the period they live in, and their messages and ideas are interpreted by coming generations according to their particular views. Literature that has been rejected by contemporary critics can become future success stories.

Elias Lönnrot collected folk poems from Finnish rune-singers, and wrote the prologue to his epic work Kalevala on February 28th, 1835. Later, the number of folk poems increased considerably, which led to the publication of a new edition of Kalevala in 1849.

The year 1999 is the Jubilee Year of Finland's national epic Kalevala, and it will also be celebrated internationally, Kalevala having been translated into about 50 languages.

Frans-Emil Sillanpää (1888–1964) is the only Finnish Literature Nobel Prize winner so far. Some of his best known novels are "Fallen Asleep While Young/The Maid Silja", "A Man's Way" and "People in the Summer Night". Sillanpää's main theme is the elevation of mankind from primitivity to awareness of human duties and purposes.

Tove Jansson's popular Moomin figures on a boat trip in the Turku archipelago (left).

Milestones in Finnish Cinema Art

The history of Finnish cinema art dates back to the first performance of the Lumière brothers on June 28th, 1896 in Helsinki. Much has happened since then. The first Finnish film-play "The Illicit Distillers" debuted in 1907. The films created in the 1930s were mostly comedies, folk-life descriptions and historical films.

Some of the best known film directors are Toivo Särkkä, Edvin Laine and Matti Kassila. After the Winter and Continuation wars, there was a boom in Finnish film-making.

The impact of television on the film industry began in 1958. The universal film crisis hit Finland, and film production stopped in 1965. But television and the importation of foreign films did not put an end to the Finnish film industry. The appreciation of and demand for domestic films soon increased, and a new generation of film directors emerged, such as Risto Jarva, Mikko Niskanen, Jaakko Pakkasvirta, Mauno Kurkvaara and Åke Lindman.

In 1969, the Finnish Film Foundation was established to arrange funding for domestic film production.

The most prominent among modern Finnish film directors are Rauni Mollberg, Timo Linnansalo, Tapio Suominen, Aki and Mika Kaurismäki and Renny Harlin, the latter being best known for his Hollywood action-films.

In 1997, Finnish films were presented at the film festivals of Venice, Berlin and Moscow. At these events, 20 prizes were awarded for Finnish productions. In the same year, Auli Mantila received international recognition for the film "Collector".

An animated Kafka-trilogy by Katariina Lillqvist and the film "Drifting Clouds" by Aki Kaurismäki have also been extremely well received abroad. In 2002, film director Aki Kaurismäki received the Grand Prix du Jury for his film "The Man without a Past". Kati Outinen, who held the leading feminine role in the film, was presented the prize for best actress.

Film producer, director and actor Åke Lindman is one of the most prominent figures in Finnish film. He has acted in many films, one of the most memorable being "The Unknown Soldier", based on the novel by Väinö Linna. The latest film directed by Lindman is "Kultala", a story about the gold fever in Lapland in the 1860s.

Film director Aki Kaurismäki at the award ceremony after having received the Grand Prix du Jury at the 55th Film Festival 2002 in Cannes.

Renny Harlin has received international fame as a director of action movies.

Famous Finnish Athletes

The legendary Paavo Nurmi (1917–1973) is unquestionably one of the most celebrated among Finnish athletes. During his active years, he won 25 world championships, 9 Olympic Gold Medals and 3 Olympic Silver Medals.

The Finns practice a wide range of sports, and are becoming increasingly successful competitors on the international arenas. Among top achievers in motor sports are Formula 1-drives Mika Häkkinen and Kimi Räikkönen and rally drives Tommi Mäkinen, Juha Kankkunen and Marcus Grönholm.

In 1995, Anne-Mari Sandell won a European Championship in long-distance running and Karoliina Lundahl celebrated a World Championship in weight lifting in the 75 kg class. During his outstanding career, swimmer Jani Sievinen has received 100 medals, most of which are golden ones. The Finnish icehockey team has been very successful, winning the World Championship in 1995 and Olympic bronze in 1998. In the 2002 Winter Olympics, Samppa Lajunen brought home 3 gold medals in Nordic Combined skiing. In the Paraolympics, Finnish athletes have received several medals over the past years. These are only a few examples of the recent success stories in the history of Finnish sports achievements.

Finland hosts many popular sporting events every year. In summer, there is the Sulkava rowing competition, the Helsinki Marathon and the traditional Jukola relay race which lasts throughout the bright summer night. Those who are looking for thrilling winter sports challenges can participate in the Pirkka ski race or the iceskating marathon in Hollola.

But everybody cannot become a top athlete. A majority of Finns, however, practice some kind of sport, and pass this habit on to their young. Schools and homes are responsible for encouraging children to practice exercise that brings them health and joy of life. Physical exercise should be a source of joy and happiness – not an exhausting daily obligation.

Finnish ice-hockey player Ville Peltonen chasing the puck during a match against Sweden in Zürich 1998.

Samuli Vasala is one of the promising young long-distance runners whose achievements spur the younger generation of athletes.

The statue of Paavo Nurmi, sculpted by Wäinö Aaltonen, is situated in front of the Helsinki Olympic Stadium. The stadium can seat 40 000 spectators. It also incorporates a Sports Museum.

The city of Lahti hosts many big international winter sports events. The famous ski-jumping hill is a part of the city's identity.

Mika Häkkinen's many victories in international Formula-competitions have made him one of the best known racing drivers in the world. These achievements are a result of hard work and "sisu", this typically Finnish form of tenacity. Besides Formula drivers Mika Häkkinen and Kimi Räikkönen, rally drivers Tommi Mäkinen, Juha Kankkunen, Marcus Grönholm and Harri Rovanperä are among the great achievers in motor sports. Finns do not give in easily. But toughness alone is not enough. Sound judgment, intelligence and ingenuity are also needed.

Events and Happenings

Finland Festivals, a joint body of Finnish art and cultural festival organisers, handles the promotion, marketing and communication of these events both at home and abroad.

Finland can offer interesting happenings for every taste during every season, from the Hanko regatta in the South to the "Suomi juoksee" (Finland runs) running event starting in Utsjoki in the North. In the southwestern archipelago, the autonomous province of land offers a multitude of interesting events throughout the summer. In the city of Oulu, off the coast of the Gulf of Bothnia, the annual "tervasoutu" (tar rowing competition) is arranged in June. This tradition bears reference to the Middle Age, when the city was a major centre for the tar trade. In southern Finland, visitors can enjoy the swinging tunes at the famous Pori jazz festival, and in the city of Rauma, famous for its drumlace work, the "week of lace" is arranged in August every year. In the historical city of Turku you can listen to rock music at the Ruisrock festival or enjoy classical music at the Turku Concert Hall. Turku is also the home town of our most famous athlete, and here the sports-minded can participate in the Paavo Nurmi marathon.

In Helsinki, there is the Helsinki Festival in late August and early September, the climax of which is the "Night of the Arts", when cultural institutions are open until the small hours. Another interesting event in Helsinki is the annual "Baltic herring market" when fishermen from different parts of the country sell fish and other products at the Helsinki Market Square. The Särkänniemi amusement park in Tampere offers summer entertainment for the whole family. Other famous summer events are the Tango Festival in Seinäjoki and the Chamber Music Festival in Kuhmo, the Music Festival in Mikkeli and the famous event "Kuopio Sings and Dances" in the city of Kuopio. In the North, you can visit the Kainuu fair in summer, and admire the world's biggest snow castle in Kemi in winter. From there, you can travel one hour by car or bus to Rovaniemi, "the gateway to Lapland". One of Lapland's most interesting events is the Feast of Mary at Hetta in Enontekiö, an annual event with long traditions, bringing the Samis together to various activities. Lapland is a unique experience, with its light summer nights when the sun never sets, and its polar night "kaamos" in winter. It is an experience that cannot be described, it must be lived.

Among religious events, there is the ecumenical council meeting, which is arranged every second year in different parts of the country, the revivalist's summer festivals and various orthodox festivities, such as the church festival called "Praasniekka".

In Finland, Midsummer night is celebrated with thousands of bonfires blazing along shores and river banks.

Festivities during the First of May are dedicated to students and workers. Students in their white caps enjoying a traditional picnic-lunch at Ullanlinna, Helsinki.

The Pori Jazz Festival in July is a popular musical event.

Finland is a country of thousands of lakes and waterways. The picture is from Kurenniemi in the city of Heinola.

The Särkänniemi amusement park in Tampere offers entertainment for the whole family. The world's biggest snow castle is built in Kemi every winter (picture on the next page, right).

Safe Journey

Travelling in Finland is safe and convenient. From the Helsinki-Vantaa international airport, domestic flights are available to destinations as far north as Ivalo in Lapland. The flight from Frankfurt to Helsinki takes 2 1/2 hours, from London 3 hours, New York 9 hours and Tokyo 9 1/2 hours. Finland's well functioning road network, multitude of service stations and comfortable hotels cater to the tourists' every need. The camping sites are open from the beginning of June until the end of August. More than 750 hotels and numerous other accommodation services offer rooms during every season. Open-air tourism services are available in most parts of the country.

A majority of the middle-aged and young population speak English besides Finnish and Swedish. The most common international credit cards are accepted in almost every business facility in the country. Via the Internet, connections can be maintained with any part of the world. Health services are available to everybody.

Due to the changing weather conditions, special attention should be paid to adequate clothing, especially in winter. This is particularly important in Lapland, where the weather can be extremely cold and the winds unrelenting.

The Finnish National Road Administration is responsible for the public roads in Finland. The roads are paved all the way from Helsinki in the South to Utsjoki in the North. The picture shows the Turku freeway (highway 1).

Finnair's blue and white aeroplanes fly passengers to practically any part of the globe. Nearly ten million people use the Helsinki-Vantaa airport every year.

Finland has an excellent railway network, and the trains are built for domestic weather conditions. The new spacious Pendolino-train traffics the line Helsinki–Turku, and will soon be used on other routes as well.

A sightseeing-cruise gives an excellent view of the Finnish archipelago.

The picturesque old sheds on the banks of the Porvoo river in the town of Porvoo is a popular tourist attraction.

Åland is an autonomous province of Finland. It consists of 6 500 islands and skerries. There is a regular maritime traffic between the Finnish mainland and land. The picture shows the Brändö archipelago.

In the outskirts of many Finnish cities there are several comfortable hotels in beautiful natural surroundings. Hotel Scandic Kajaani in northeastern Finland near the Kajaani river has 235 rooms and five saunas.

The luxury Spa Hotel Casino in Savonlinna is ideally located on the shore of lake Haapavesi, belonging to he Saimaa lake system.

The Tampere Spa is a diversified health spa and a luxury hotel. Most of the rooms are equipped with a sauna or a yacuzzi, and the spa can offer a multitude of health and beauty treatment services. The swimming-pool temperature is tropical, + 30°C.

The Punkaharju Natural Park near the city of Savonlinna is famous for its beautiful ridges covered with pine trees. One of the most popular tourist attractions of Punkaharju is the Retretti Cultural Centre, offering visitors a great variety of art exhibitions and concerts.

The hotel Imatran Valtionhotelli was built in 1903. It is one of Finland's finest "Art Nouveau" buildings, designed by architect Usko Nyström. The hotel is situated near the Imatra rapids in the city of Imatra in southeastern Finland.

The Concert and Congress House Mikaeli in the city of Mikkeli is designed by Arto Sipinen. It is an ideal venue for many kinds of cultural and professional events.

The town of Lappajärvi in Ostrobothnia has been built on the crater of a meteor. Here, the Kivitippu Spa offers conference services, holiday packages and different kinds of treatments, as well as an interesting meteorite exhibition.

During the last few years, golf has become a very popular sport in Finland, and a great number of golf courses have been built in different parts of the country. Information about golfing possibilities is available from the Finnish Golf Association and the Finnish Golf Magazine (Suomen Golflehti).

The Bengtskär lighthouse, built of granite and bricks, was completed in 1906. This popular tourist attraction is situated about 20 kilometers off the southwestern coast of Finland. It is highest lighthouse in Scandinavia.

Travelling along the countryside is a rewarding way of getting to know the rural parts of Finland. A Finnish company called 4H-Rural Holidays (Maaseutulomat) has been developing this kind of tourism for thirty years. They can offer accommodation for children, adults and families in cabins, farm houses and camp schools.

Many Finns dream about a summer cottage by the sea or near a lake.There are about 450 000 summer cottages in Finland, the majority of which are fit for winter habitation. Most Finns take their vacation in July, when the Finnish summer is at its loveliest.

In Finland, the tourist can find rural idylls close to urban environments, or even in cities. This cabin is situated in Bemböle in the city of Espoo.

Finnish Food Culture

Traditionally, the Finnish food economy was based on products from farming and animal husbandry, and on hunting and fishing. The past decades have seen a considerable change and diversification of Finnish gastronomy.

But still today it is possible to encounter provincial specialities in many parts of the country. The province of Savo is known for its "kalakukko", or baked fish loaf. The fish, mostly vendace, is baked with pork in a crust made of rye dough. Karelian pasties (karjalanpiirakka), thin oval shaped pies with rice or potato filling, and Karelian beef ragout (karjalanpaisti) are typically Karelian dishes. An Ostrobothnian delicacy is "leipäjuusto", a special home-made cheese, often served with cloudberries. In Lapland's speciality "poronkäristys" or reindeer ragout, thin strips of frozen reindeer are simmered in a pot, seasoned, and eaten with lingonberry or cranberry jelly. Traditional southwestern foods are pickled fish rolls made of baltic herring, and pork gravy, which is also very popular in the province of Häme. A speciality of the province of Uusimaa is potato sausages consisting of lean pork, beef and mashed potatoes. Åland is famous for its delicious black bread. The traditional food in the Finnish archipelago is, of course, fish, mostly baltic herring, perch, pike or bream.

Sausages, fried or grilled over an open fire, is the most popular food in Finland, and in cities and other urban environments, hamburger and pizza restaurants have replaced many small restaurants offering traditional Finnish food.

The table-setting skills of Finnish chefs can be admired in the charming brick-vaulted premises of Fregatti Oy, a well-known Finnish catering enterprise in Katajanokka, Helsinki (right).

The beautiful Finnish summer offers ideal conditions for picnics and parties in the open air.

The shingle roof of the Petäjävesi wooden church is made by hand. The church was built in 1763–1765 by the self-learned folk master Jaakko Leppänen. In 1994, the church was included in Unesco's World Heritage List.

Kalevala Koru brings back the splendour of ancient times. Their hand-made jewellery combines old traditions with oriental mysticism and the latest trends in the occidental fashion world. The picture shows a snake-motif brooch.

This beautiful hand-made doll was found at the Helsinki Market Place.

The Finnish knife, "puukko", is a traditional working tool, but also a highly valued tourist souvenir.

The Finnish Handicraft Tradition

The handicraft tradition, earlier threathened by industrial manufacture, is regaining popularity. Today, the offspring of ancient Finnish church masters and craftsmen have good possibilities to become skilled handicraft professionals themselves. The basic skills are normally taught in the homes.

Finland has 40 schools and institutes teaching arts and crafts. They provide diversified training in handling different kinds of materials. People graduated from handicraft schools are called "artesans," whereas those who have received a college-level diploma are called "artenomes". The Finnish Handicraft Museum in Jyväskylä is responsible for the country's handicraft museums. The Luostarinmäki Handicraft Museum in Turku, opened in 1940, is a unique 18th century artisans' town.

Linen is a traditional Finnish clothing fabric. Natural fibres and colours are again highly valued. Finnish turf is another environment-friendly and solid clothing material.

Handicraft is an important part of Finnish creativity, folk tradition and professionalism, and it will certainly maintain its position in the future.

The interior decoration of the Petäjävesi church is still the same as in the 1760s.

A fishnet-mender demonstrating traditional skills at the Seurasaari Open Air Museum in Helsinki.

Sightseeing in Finland

Finland can offer many interesting tourist attractions, from Åland's beautiful groves in the South to the Utsjoki church in the North. The Suomenlinna sea-fortress, built on a group of islands outside Helsinki, is an important monument of fortress architecture. The building of this stately stronghold began in 1747. The medieval castles of Turku, Hämeenlinna and Olavinlinna are popular historical monuments and sights.

One of the most visited sights of Helsinki is the Sibelius-monument, sculpted by Professor Eila Hiltunen.

In the outskirts of Helsinki there are many interesting places to visit, one being the unique wilderness of the Nuuksio National Park.

Finland can offer a multitude of architectural sights, from the old Petäjävesi church to the modern building of Kiasma, the Museum of Contemporary Art.

Old urban cultures are represented by the romantic old city of Porvoo, with its picturesque wooden houses and sheds, and Old Rauma, the medieval old town of the city of Rauma in southwestern Finland.

The interminable reaches and snowcovered peaks of Lapland is an unforgettable experience for many visitors.

In Finland, the seasonal changes give the landscape dramatically varying colours and shades. The blue lakes and green forests of the summer are transformed into a white infinity in winter. Our beautiful natural parks continue to fascinate foreign visitors during every season.

The construction of the Hämeenlinna Castle was begun in the 1260s. The castle, situated in the city of Hämeenlinna, is a popular tourist attraction.

Finland's highest waterfall is Hepokängäs, with a drop of about 24 metres. It lies between Puolanka and Hyrynsalmi.

One of the best known attractions in Helsinki is the Lutheran cathedral designed by C.L. Engel, and completed in 1852. The cathedral and the Senate square are part of the unique Empire-quarter in the centre of Helsinki.

An enchanting view from the sea near the Helsinki harbour, showing the Olympia quay and the Helsinki Observatory .

The outstandingly original Temppeliaukio Church in Helsinki, built in the rock, is visited by half a million tourists every year.

The Market Place and the Uspenski cathedral seen from the Helsinki harbour. The Sibelius monument, the Railway Station and the Paavo Nurmi statue can be reached from the harbour by foot, tram or bus.

The Helsinki Railway Station, designed by Eliel Saarinen, is a rare example of neo-romantic architecture. It was completed in 1914.

Finland's Ever Changing Natural Scenery

Finland's solid granite bedrock was liberated from the glaciers only about 11 000 years ago. Erratic blocks and pot holes still remind us of this period. With the melting of the ice masses, 188.000 lakes emerged, so the saying that Finland is the "land of thousand lakes" is a slight understatement. The biggest lakes are Lake Saimaa in southeastern Finland and Lake Inari in Lapland.

Kemijoki is the longest of Finland's fairly short and shallow rivers. In order to preserve the variety of the Finnish landscape, even small brooks and swamps are nowadays under protection. About 70% of the country's surface area consists of virgin forests. About 10% of the forest land is protected, an area corresponding to the total cultivated land area. Finland consist mainly of lowlands, but there are considerable local height differences. In northern Lapland you can find the country's most impressive fells, of wich Haltiatunturi is the highest (1 328 metres). About 25% of the country's total area is marshland, of which a part is protected under the Natura programme.

Among the tree species thriving in southern Finland are oak, maple and alder, whereas spruce and Lapp birch can survive in the North. Spruce, birch, alder and aspen are common species in the whole country. The vegetation varies considerably, and treeless areas can be found only in the northern fell regions.

The seasonal changes are remarkable. In Lapland, the temperature can be about -40°C, whereas the summers can be extremely warm, with record temperatures of about +30°C. These are extreme variations, and the medium temperatures are much more moderate.

The Aallokkokoski rapids of the Kitkajoki river in Kuusamo is part of the Oulanka National Park. The best known trekking-route in this park is the 95 km "Karhunkierros" (Bear path) (right).

Autumn colours in a wood grove in the city of Espoo.

The bristled seal of lake Saimaa is a unique endangered arctic species, and one of the rarest animals in the world. About one hundred and fifty of them have survived so far.

In Finland there are over two hundred native bird species and about 60 different mammals. Bears and wolves are among the best known large predators. The arctic fox is near extinction. The largest mammal is the elk, of which there are about 300.000 specimens. Caribou are found in northeastern Finland, and reindeer in Lapland.

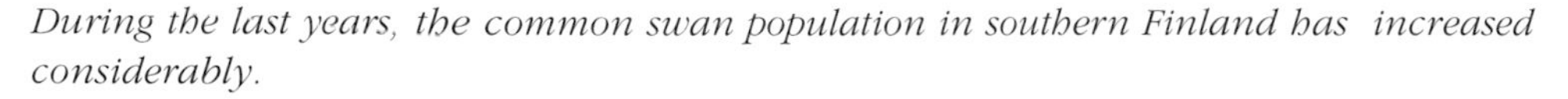

During the last years, the common swan population in southern Finland has increased considerably.

The wolf is an endangered species in Finland. Originally, wolves are social herd animals, but nowadays their freedom is restricted and their natural instincts have been disturbed (left).

In Finland Everyman's Right is applied, which gives you the right to roam freely in the open air, as long as you do not harm the environment or light fires in places where this is forbidden. As a member of the European Union, Finland aims at preserving its flora and fauna in accordance with the regulations of the Natura Programme. We are all responsible for preserving the diversity of our environment.

The National Park of Nuuksio is one of Europe´s last wilderness regions. These protected areas are as important to the people of the year 2000 as they have been to earlier generations.

Sunset at Ristikallio in Kuusamo.

A view from the Kangasala ridge to lake Vesijärvi, Längelmävesi.

Fishing in the Kuusamo rapids.

Finland has over 30 National Parks and about 20 Natural Parks. In addition to these, there are many other protected areas for hikers and other open-air enthusiasts.

The Koli National Park lies in northern Karelia. Its highest mountain, Ukko-Koli, rises 235 metres above the surface of Lake Pielisjärvi.

The Oulanka National Park in Kainuu in northeastern Finland is a unique wilderness with barren wastelands and untamed watercourses. Further north are Lapland's magic fells, where you can meet Lapp dogs watching over reindeer herds.

Lapland and the Samis

The Sami population occupies northern territories in Norway, Sweden, Finland and Russia. They have their own culture and their own language. In Finland, there are three different Sami languages: North Sami, Inari Sami and Skolt Sami. North Sami is the standard language and the common language for the Nordic Samis.

The Finnish Samis live in the districts of Enontekiö, Inari and Utsjoki as well as in the Vuotso region of the Sodankylä district. The Finnish Sami population amounts to about 7 000 persons, of which 2/3 live in the Sami districts.

The most important symbols of the Sami culture are their own flag and their own costume (Sámi gákti). The Sami culture can be studied in Inari, in the Sami Museum, Siida, and in the Arktikum-centre in Rovaniemi.

The county of Lapland has over 200.000 inhabitants. Its capital, Rovaniemi, is a vigorous centre for trade and tourism. Lapland's university is situated in Rovaniemi. Besides an important brewing industry, there are different primary and processing industries. Tourism is, however, the most important livelihood for the Lapps.

You can find gold in the rivers of Lapland. Gold washers try their luck at Lemmenjoki, Morgamoja and Tankavaara, but in spite of the hard effort the result is usually very meagre.

The Sami handicraft products are colourful as well as practical.

The serenity and silence of Lapland's national and natural parks help people to gather strength for future challenges.

Lapland offers spectacular views and unforgettable experiences. Santa Claus, who lives at Korvatunturi in Lapland, is known by children all over the world, and by adults as well.

Finnish Lapland can offer a multitude of exotic tourist attractions. One of them is the Pallastunturi fells and Hotel Pallas. In Rovaniemi, there is the Arktikum-centre, incorporating the Provincial Museum of Lapland, and the Lappia-house, designed by Alvar Aalto. Tourists usually stop to buy souvenirs and take snapshots at the demarcation line of the Arctic Circle. A bit further away is the Santa Park, and still further the Sami museum, Siida.

The Siberian jay (kuukkeli) is a mysterious and very curious bird. It often stops to marvel at the behaviour of us humans. Below, winter kaamos twilight at Karigasniemi. In the background, the Ailigastunturi fell.

The tourists looking for peace and quiet will enjoy a visit to the Kätkä-cabin at Muotkavaara. In February, the infinity of the crusted, glittering snow is an unforgettable experience.

During starlit winter nights, the sky is illuminated by the breathtaking Northern Lights (Aurora borealis). The picture to the left shows the dark silhouette of the Nammalkuru wilderness cabin.

A skier in the Pallas-Ounastunturi National Park.

Finland and the European Union

Finland participates actively in the decision making of all the important instances of the European Union. The common EU monetary unit, Euro, guarantees a solid and secure development of the national economy.

As a member of EU, our country participates in the preparation of development programmes for Russia and other European countries, as well as in their implementation, especially through the programme "Nordic Dimension" launched by Finland. The EU-membership is also an important security factor for Finland.

The Finnish representative office of the EU-commission is situated in Pohjoisesplanadi street in Helsinki.

Facts about Finland

Population: 5 194 901 (31.12.2001)
Average population density: 17 inh./sq.km, in Lapland 2,2/sq.km.
Average annual population growth: 0,3%
Life expectancy: Women 80,5 years, men 73 years
Constitution: Republic
Languages: Finnish, Swedish (6%) and Sami in the Sami regions.
English is taught in schools as a first foreign language
Religions: Evangelical Lutheran 85 %, Orthodox 1 %
Location: Between 60 and 70 degrees northern latitude
Longest distance from the south to the north: 1160 km,
and from the west to the east: 540 km
Time: + 2 h compared to GMT
Average temperature: Helsinki; February, -6°C, July, +16°C
Sodankylä (Lapland); January, -14°C, July +14,4°C
National day: 6.12. (Independence Day)
Monetary Unit: Euro. 1 Euro = 100 cent
Population in the biggest cities (31.12.2001)
Helsinki: 559 718 (capital)
Espoo 216 836
Tampere 197 774
Vantaa 179 856
Turku 173 686
Oulu 123 274
Lahti 97 543
Kuopio 87 347
Jyväskylä 80 372
Pori 75 995
Lappeenranta 58 401
Vaasa 57 014
Kotka 54 768
Joensuu 52 140

Raimo Suikkari, Poet and Photographer

Already as a child, Raimo Suikkari loved to ramble in the beautiful Finnish woods and forests. His deep feeling for the natural scenery inspired him to write poetry and to eternalize fascinating sights through his camera lens. As a romantic, he never stops admiring the beauty and miracles of Nature. He has photographed the Finnnish landscape from Espoo in the South to Utsjoki in the North, but sites like the Malaysian jungle, Hawaii or the Masai Mara Natural Park in Kenya are not unfamiliar to him and his camera.

Raimo Suikkari is a member of the Board of Directors of the Espoo Writers' Association. His book "Vihreän planeetan kutsu" (The call of the green planet) is an interesting dream fantasy about a better future. His literary production reflects open-mindedness, serenity, love and joy of life. His illustrated Finland-books have been translated into nearly a dozen languages, and published in several editions.

Katri Sarmavuori

Earlier publications by Raimo Suikkari:

Sininen rakkaus, poems, 1992
Suomen luontokuvia, 1992
Sininen unelma, poems 1993
Suomea Helsingistä Lappiin, 1993
(awarded a certificate of honour)
Vihreän Planeetan kutsu, 1993
Helsinki-Kirja 1994
Sininen uni, poems 1995
Finland 2000, 1996
Your Friend Finland, 1997
Sininen hiljaisuus, poems 1997
Beautiful Finnish Lapland, 1997
Helsinki, Espoo ja Vantaa 1998
Runokuvia Suomen Lapista/Poetic Images of Finnish Lapland 1999
Enkelihiutaleita 2000
Nähtävyyksien Suomi 2000
Helsinki Sights and Attractions 2001
Suomi vuodenaikojen sinfonia 2001
Nuuksion laulu/The Song of Finland 2002

Time Zones